IT'S TIME TO EAT A RED BANANA

It's Time to Eat a Red Banana

Walter the Educator

Silent King Books
A WhichHead Entertainment Imprint

Copyright © 2024 by Walter the Educator

All rights reserved. No part of this book may be reproduced in any manner whatsoever without written per- mission except in the case of brief quotations embodied in critical articles and reviews.

First Printing, 2024

Disclaimer

This book is a literary work; the story is not about specific persons, locations, situations, and/or circumstances unless mentioned in a historical context. Any resemblance to real persons, locations, situations, and/or circumstances is coincidental. This book is for entertainment and informational purposes only. The author and publisher offer this information without warranties expressed or implied. No matter the grounds, neither the author nor the publisher will be accountable for any losses, injuries, or other damages caused by the reader's use of this book. The use of this book acknowledges an understanding and acceptance of this disclaimer.

It's Time to Eat a Red Banana is a collectible early learning book by Walter the Educator suitable for all ages belonging to Walter the Educator's Time to Eat Book Series. Collect more books at WaltertheEducator.com

USE THE EXTRA SPACE TO TAKE NOTES AND DOCUMENT YOUR MEMORIES

RED BANANA

It's time to eat, what's that I see?

It's Time to Eat a Red Banana

A red banana waiting for me!

Not yellow like the ones I know,

This one's red with a special glow!

From the tropics, warm and bright,

Where the sun shines day and night,

This red banana grew so tall,

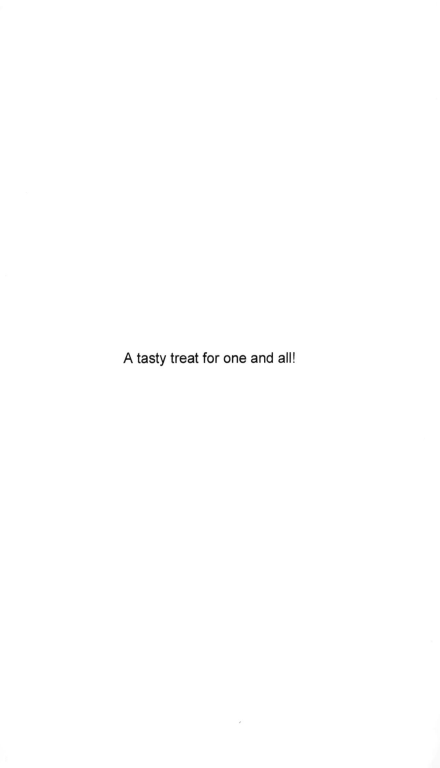
A tasty treat for one and all!

Oh, red banana, sweet and new,

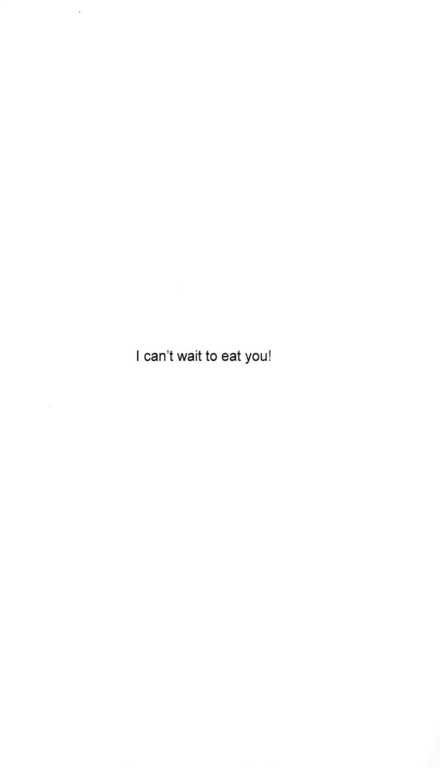

I can't wait to eat you!

Soft and creamy, what a treat,

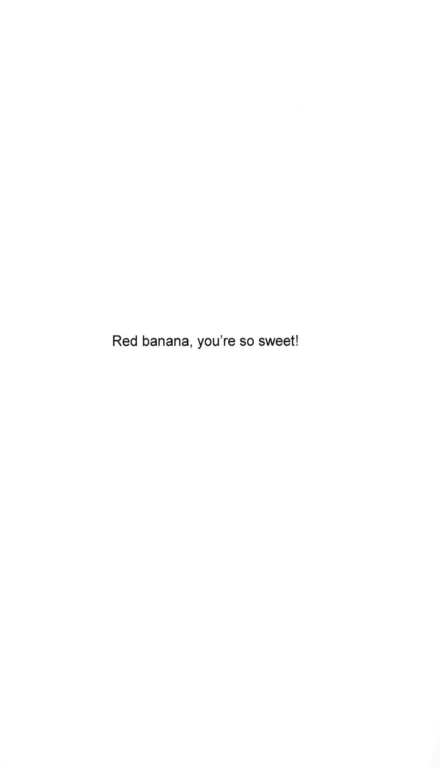

Red banana, you're so sweet!

I peel you slowly, just like so,

And what's inside? A creamy show!

Not too big, not too small,

You're just the right size for me to hold and call!

It's Time to Eat a
Red
Banana

I take a bite, oh, what a taste!

Soft and mild, no time to waste!

You're sweet like honey, smooth like cream,

Eating you feels like a dream!

Oh, red banana, sweet and new,

I can't wait to eat you!

Soft and creamy, what a treat,

Red banana, you're so sweet!

Your skin is red, like a sunset sky,

A special fruit that's bold and shy.

Inside, you're golden, soft, and bright,

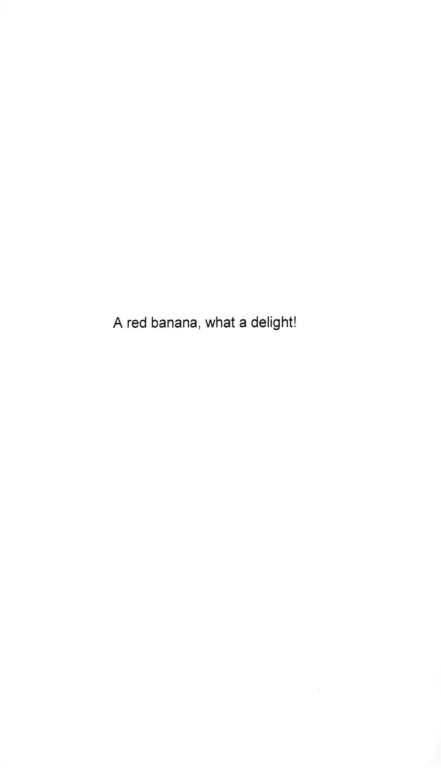
A red banana, what a delight!

You're full of flavor, soft and rich,

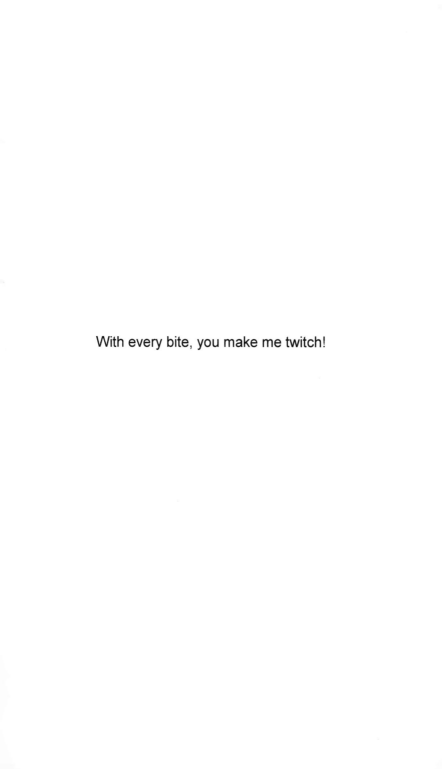
With every bite, you make me twitch!

A fruity snack I love to eat,

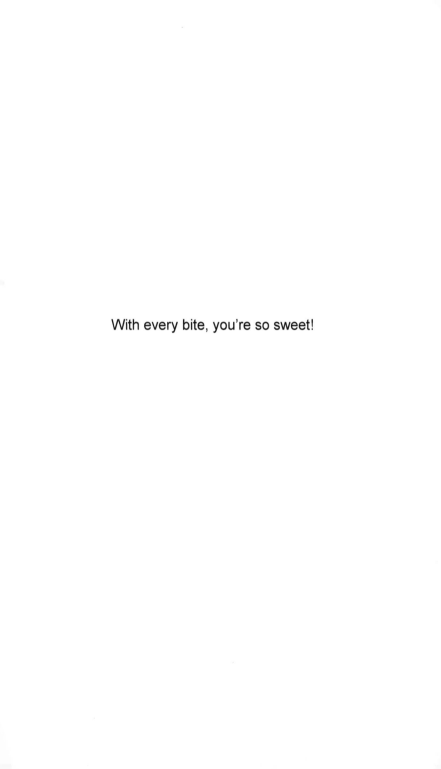

With every bite, you're so sweet!

Sometimes you're in smoothies or bread,

Or just on a plate, all shiny and red.

You're good for breakfast, or any time,

It's Time to Eat a

Red Banana

Red banana, you're so fine!

Oh, red banana, sweet and new,

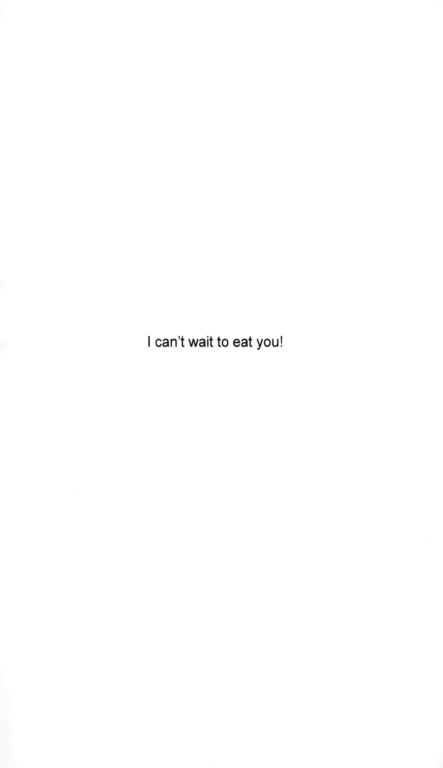

I can't wait to eat you!

Soft and creamy, what a treat,

Red banana, you're so sweet!

ABOUT THE CREATOR

Walter the Educator is one of the pseudonyms for Walter Anderson. Formally educated in Chemistry, Business, and Education, he is an educator, an author, a diverse entrepreneur, and he is the son of a disabled war veteran. "Walter the Educator" shares his time between educating and creating. He holds interests and owns several creative projects that entertain, enlighten, enhance, and educate, hoping to inspire and motivate you. Follow, find new works, and stay up to date with Walter the Educator™

at WaltertheEducator.com

Milton Keynes UK
Ingram Content Group UK Ltd.
UKHW021938281024
450365UK00018B/1150